Soups

C H E S A P E A K E   B A Y

SOUPS

Whitey Schmidt

*"There is a well-worn controversy among chowder lovers
as to which is correct, the kind made with milk
or the kind made with tomato and water . . .
Who knows? Furthermore, who cares?
You should eat according to your own tastes
as much as possible, and if you want to make a chowder
with milk and tomato, crackers and potatoes,
do it, if the result pleases you
(which sounds somewhat doubtful, but possible)."*

M.F.K. FISHER

•

Printed in the
United States of America
Second Printing, 2010
ISBN 978-0-9613008-6-9

Library of Congress Control Number 2007900925

© 2007 by Marian Hartnett Press
Box 88, Crisfield, Maryland 21817

Designed by Sue Knopf, Graffolio

Contents

Introduction

Chesapeake Bay soups provide sustenance and satisfaction in generous measure. The simple skills needed to make these soups are easily mastered, and the opportunities for personal creativity are abundant. Soup is among the most satisfying of foods—it nourishes both the soul and the body. I know that in my own home and studio, nothing gives me more pleasure than a pot of soup simmering away on the back burner of the stove.

Soup is also one of the most fundamental forms of food. Its traditions go back to the earliest days of Chesapeake history. A Chesapeake soup may serve as a single course of a meal or may be its centerpiece—rounded out with good bread and a green salad. If you're planning an elegant menu, a Chesapeake soup makes a good starter, for many of them have just the subtle flavor needed to complement a complex main course. There are also times when soup is *it*—I'll select three soups and let them be my whole meal.

As the great variety of recipes in this book shows, soup-making can transform a group of nourishing ingredients into a dish that's more than the sum of its parts. The favorite Chesapeake soups are based on crabmeat, clams, oysters, fish, and fresh-from-the-garden vegetables. They're hearty mélanges that have nourished and gladdened generations of Chesapeake natives. These flavorful, exuberant dishes are characterized by the Bay's agricultural history and proximity to the water, and some have been handed down from family members for generations.

The great soups of the Chesapeake—great by virtue of both their popularity and the number of variations that exist—are oyster stews and crab soups. One of the most popular is the *Maryland Vegetable Crab Soup*, which uses vegetables for interest and color, crabmeat for sweetness, and spices to entice. *Cream of Crab Soup*, on the other hand, is laden with cream and butter and splashed with an elegant garnish of sherry.

Chesapeake soups come from a diversity of rich food traditions. To present the best, I have worked with talented cooks and many other sources encountered in my Chesapeake travels, such as restaurants, markets, crab houses, and crab shanties. I'm proud to offer a selection of the best new and time-honored recipes of the Bay region.

Get cookin'!

Whitey Schmidt

The Basics of Soup Making

The basis of most soups is a well-made stock created by simmering meat or bones, a chicken carcass, shrimp shells, crab shells—even fish heads and bones—with aromatic vegetables and herbs. While you can buy ready-made stocks or cubes to cut down on cooking time, a rich homemade stock with fresh ingredients undoubtedly has an edge over a store-bought one.

Baltimore Beef Stock

2 quarts water

2 pounds beef bones—
    shoulder, top ribs, etc.

2 leeks, sliced

2 onions, sliced

2 carrots, sliced

1 rib celery, peeled and
    sliced

2 potatoes, peeled and
    sliced

4 garlic cloves, minced

2 bay leaves

1 sprig thyme

4 whole cloves

8 black peppercorns

6 sprigs parsley

salt to taste

Pour the water into a large soup pot and add the bones, leeks, onions, carrots, celery, potatoes, garlic, and spices. Bring to a boil; then reduce heat, cover, and simmer for 3 to 4 hours, stirring occasionally. Remove the bones and strain the broth through a fine sieve, collecting the vegetables and leaving the broth clear.

Makes about 2 quarts.

Eastern Shore Chicken Stock

3–4 pounds chicken
    bones, cooked or
    uncooked

3 quarts water

5 garlic cloves, skins left
    on and lightly bruised

4 ounces mushrooms,
    sliced

2 carrots, scraped and
    roughly chopped

2 onions, quartered

2 ribs celery, peeled and
    chopped

1 leek, roughly sliced

4 sprigs parsley

4 sprigs thyme

2 bay leaves

10 black peppercorns

salt

Put the chicken bones in a stockpot with the water and bring slowly to a boil. Skim off any scum and add the garlic, mushrooms, carrots, onions, celery, leek, parsley, thyme, bay leaves, peppercorns, and salt. Bring back to a boil, reduce the heat, and partially cover the pot. Simmer gently for 2½ to 3 hours. Strain through a fine sieve, taste, adjust the seasoning, and allow to cool. Mop up any fat from the surface with a folded paper towel or refrigerate until fat has hardened and can be lifted off.

Makes about 2 quarts.

There are differences between fish stocks and other stocks. For one thing, not all fish is suitable for stock, at least not for general purposes; stick with the heads and bones of white, mild-flavored fish. I also use shrimp and crab shells.

Northern Neck Fish Stock

4 pounds assorted fish heads, skeletons, and scraps

shrimp and crab shells

3 or 4 tomatoes, roughly chopped

1 large onion, quartered

2 ribs celery, peeled and cut into chunks

3 cloves garlic

10 peppercorns

2 bay leaves

2 or 3 sprigs fresh thyme

1/2 cup roughly chopped fresh parsley

2 tablespoons extra-virgin olive oil

1 cup dry white wine

salt and freshly ground black pepper

1/2 lemon, rind and all

4 quarts water

Combine all ingredients in a stockpot. Bring almost to a boil; then partially cover and adjust the heat so that the mixture sends up a few bubbles at a time. Cook at a slow simmer for 45 minutes. Strain through a fine sieve, then taste and add salt if necessary.

Makes about 3 quarts.

Tidewater Vegetable Stock

2 onions, roughly chopped

2 large carrots, roughly chopped

2 ribs celery, peeled and roughly chopped

2 leeks, roughly sliced

4 ounces mushrooms, sliced

2 cloves garlic, chopped

handful of fresh parsley, stems included

1 teaspoon sea salt

8 black peppercorns

3 quarts cold water

Place onions, carrots, celery, leeks, mushrooms, garlic, parsley, salt, and peppercorns in a stockpot. Add cold water. Place over medium-high heat and bring to a boil. Reduce heat to medium-low and simmer for 1 to 1 1/2 hours, removing scum from the surface occasionally. Strain through a fine sieve, then taste and add salt if necessary.

Makes about 2 quarts.

Clam Chowders

Miles River
Clam Chowder

Bohemia River
Clam Chowder

Choptank River
Clam Chowder

Pocomoke River
Clam Chowder

Sassafras River
Clam & Corn Chowder

Tred Avon River
Clam & Basil Chowder

Miles River Clam Chowder

A rich and delicious first course, clam chowder makes a marvelous start to any meal. Serve with lots of crusty bread. This soup is similar to a chunky veggie style. Marjoram, thyme, and parsley give it a wonderful taste.

50 chowder clams

1 cup water

4 small potatoes, peeled and diced

1/4 pound green beans, chopped

1 green pepper, chopped

4 small carrots, chopped

3 ears corn, kernels removed

2 large onions, chopped

3 ribs celery, peeled and chopped

1 can tomatoes, chopped

1 can tomato soup

1 tablespoon fresh sweet marjoram

1 teaspoon fresh thyme, chopped

1/2 teaspoon freshly ground black
    pepper

2 tablespoons butter

chopped fresh parsley

Place scrubbed clams in a pot with 1 cup water. Cover tightly and steam until open. Chop clams (discard shells and hard part) and set aside. Reserve the clam juice to use as stock. Add the potatoes, beans, green pepper, carrots, onions, celery, tomatoes, and soup and simmer until vegetables start to soften. Add corn, clams, marjoram, thyme and black pepper.

Before serving, add butter and fresh parsley.

Serves 4.

Bohemia River Clam Chowder

The day after I made this chowder, my friend Glenn Linton stopped by and said, "I'm not big on clam chowder." He ate two bowls and was looking for a third.

2 slices bacon, chopped

¼ cup chopped onion

3 ribs celery, peeled and diced

1 large green pepper, chopped

1 pint whole tomatoes

3 cups water

12 medium clams, coarsely chopped, with juice

1 teaspoon oregano

1 teaspoon thyme

½ teaspoon freshly ground black pepper

1½ pounds potatoes, peeled and diced (¼-inch dice)

Simmer the bacon, onion, celery, green pepper, and tomatoes in the 3 cups water. In a separate pot, simmer the chopped clams in their juice with the oregano, thyme, and black pepper. Combine the bacon mixture and the clams, add the diced potatoes, and simmer until the potatoes are fork tender.

Serves 4.

Crab Lab Tip

Serve a Chesapeake Bay soup as an appetizer before a main course or to balance a light meal of pasta or a sandwich. A soup can also be a meal in itself, requiring only a slice of home-baked bread to make a satisfying repast. Oh—and don't forget to serve it with a nice glass of chilled white wine.

Choptank River Clam Chowder

"Chowder for breakfast, and chowder for dinner, and chowder for supper, till you began to look for fish-bones coming through your clothes." —HERMAN MELVILLE, *MOBY DICK*, 1851

3/4 cup finely diced salt pork

1 large rib celery, peeled and chopped

1 large leek, white and pale green parts only, rinsed and chopped

1 medium onion, chopped

6 cups bottled clam juice; use the clam liquor as part of this quantity

4 cups water

4 to 5 cups peeled and diced potatoes (1½ pounds)

4 cups chopped clams

2 teaspoons chopped fresh thyme

2 tablespoons chopped fresh parsley

salt and freshly ground black pepper

Cook the salt pork in a large soup pot over medium-low heat until the fat is rendered and the pork bits are crispy, about 15 minutes. Remove the pork with a slotted spoon and drain on paper towels, leaving the drippings in the pan.

Add the celery, leek, and onion to the pan drippings and cook, stirring frequently, until the vegetables begin to soften, about 6 minutes. Add the clam juice, water, potatoes, clams, and thyme. Bring to a boil, reduce the heat to medium-low, and cook, covered, until the potatoes are tender, about 15 minutes. Remove from the heat and let the chowder rest, partially covered, at room temperature, for 1 hour.

Reheat gently. Adjust the liquid if necessary. Add more water if too thick, or simmer for a few minutes to reduce if too thin. Stir in the parsley and season to taste with salt and pepper. Pass the crisp pork bits to sprinkle on top.

Serves 6.

Pocomoke River Clam Chowder

The addition of cornstarch and evaporated milk give body to this chowder, finished with a decoration of fresh thyme just picked from the herb garden.

1 small onion, chopped

1 pint chopped clams, undrained

1 bottle (8 ounces) clam juice

1 can (16 ounces) chicken broth

1 large potato, peeled and diced

1/4 teaspoon freshly ground black pepper

1/4 cup cornstarch

1 can evaporated milk, divided

1/4 cup chopped fresh parsley

1 teaspoon dried thyme

In a soup pot, combine the onion, clams in their juice, clam juice, chicken broth, potato, and pepper; cover and bring to a boil over high heat. Cook, covered, until the potatoes are tender, 12 to 15 minutes.

In a small bowl, dissolve the cornstarch in 1/2 cup evaporated milk; add to the soup. Add the remaining evaporated milk, the parsley, and the thyme; cook, stirring frequently, until thickened—about 5 minutes.

Serves 6.

Sassafras River Clam & Corn Chowder

This thick and creamy chowder makes a satisfying supper. Finish off the meal with a tossed green salad and slices of your favorite bakery bread.

1 pint whipping cream

1 stick butter

1 large onion, finely chopped

1 apple, cored, peeled, and thinly sliced

½ teaspoon mild curry powder

2 cloves garlic, crushed

½ teaspoon cardamon

2 ears fresh corn, kernels removed

1 pound cooked new potatoes

24 boiled baby (pearl) onions

5 cups clam juice

1 pint chopped clams, poached

salt and freshly ground black pepper

6 lime wedges for garnish

Pour the cream into a small pan and cook over high heat until it is reduced by half. In a larger pan, melt half the butter. Add the onion, apple, garlic, cardamon and curry powder. Sauté until the onion is translucent. Add the reduced cream and stir well.

In another pan, melt the remaining butter and add the corn, potatoes, and onions. Cook for 5 minutes. Increase the heat and add the cream mixture and the clam juice. Bring to a boil.

Add the clams. Season well to taste with salt and pepper. Serve garnished with lime wedges.

Serves 6.

Tred Avon River Clam & Basil Chowder

When I asked my friend Chris Abbott what he thought of this soup, he said, "It's damn good!" I'll bet you'll think so too.

1½ teaspoons extra-virgin olive oil

1 medium onion, finely chopped

leaves from 1 fresh or dried sprig of thyme, chopped

2 cloves garlic, chopped

6 fresh basil leaves, chopped, plus extra for garnish

½ teaspoon crushed red chilies

4 cups clam juice

1 cup chicken stock

1½ cups strained tomatoes

1 teaspoon granulated sugar

salt and freshly ground black pepper

1 cup fresh peas, poached

⅓ cup small pasta shapes, such as penne rigate, broken into pieces

1 pint chopped clams

Heat the oil in a large pan, add the finely chopped onion, and cook gently until softened but not browned, about 5 minutes. Add the thyme, garlic, basil leaves, and chilies. Add the clam juice, chicken stock, tomatoes, and sugar along with salt and pepper to taste. Bring to a boil and then reduce to a simmer for 15 minutes, stirring occasionally. Add the peas and cook for 5 more minutes.

Add the pasta and bring to a boil again. Lower the heat and simmer for about 5 minutes or according to the pasta package instructions, stirring frequently, until the pasta is *al dente.*

Reduce the heat to low, add the clams, and heat for 10 to 12 minutes. Serve hot in warmed bowls, garnished with basil leaves.

Serves 6

Crab Soups

Rhode River
Cream of Crab Soup

Wicomico River
Crab Stew

West River Vegetable
Crab Soup

Potomac River
Crab Soup

Port Tobacco River
Crab Soup

St. Marys River
Crab Bisque

Rhode River Cream of Crab Soup

In my travels around Bay Country, I've eaten soup in every restaurant that has a view of the water. If they only had vegetable crab soup, I ate that. If they offered both styles, I ate both. Somebody had to do it.

½ stick butter

1 small onion, finely diced

¼ cup minced shallots

2 tablespoons flour

2 cups fish stock

2 cups whipping cream

1 teaspoon Worcestershire sauce

1 teaspoon salt

⅛ teaspoon white pepper

1 bay leaf

dash of Tabasco sauce

1 pound crabmeat

¼ cup sherry

lightly whipped cream and paprika for garnish

Melt the butter in a soup pot over low heat and sauté the onion and shallots until tender. Whisk in the flour and cook over medium heat, stirring constantly, for about 2 minutes. Do not brown the flour. Remove from the heat and whisk in the stock and cream.

Return to heat and stir frequently until the mixture thickens, about 10 minutes. Add the Worcestershire sauce, salt, pepper, bay leaf, Tabasco sauce, crabmeat, and sherry. Lower the heat and simmer for 20 minutes. Remove the bay leaf, ladle into warmed soup bowls, top with whipped cream and garnish with paprika.

Serves 6.

Wicomico River Crab Stew

Sometimes when I make this stew I serve it over a cup of hot rice. Mmmm. You can't have too much crabmeat in it. My son Matt said, "It's dad-gummed good."

12 female crabs, cleaned and halved, legs and claws removed

1 can (6 ounces) tomato paste

1 stick butter, melted

2 cans (8 ounces) tomato sauce

2 cups hot water

2 cups sliced onions

1 cup peeled, diced celery

½ cup diced bell peppers

1 tablespoon minced garlic

1 tablespoon Worcestershire sauce

2 tablespoons sugar

1 bay leaf

salt and freshly ground black pepper to taste

Tabasco sauce to taste

1 pound lump crabmeat

Rinse halved crabs well and set aside. In a heavy-bottomed Dutch oven, brown tomato paste over medium-high heat. Blend in melted butter, tomato sauce, and water. Cook until mixture simmers. Add onion, celery, bell peppers, and garlic. Simmer 10 minutes and add Worcestershire sauce, sugar, and bay leaf.

Add halved crabs to sauce and simmer approximately 1 hour. Additional water may be added if mixture becomes too thick. Season with salt, pepper, and Tabasco sauce. When flavor is fully developed, gently fold in lump crabmeat. Adjust seasonings if necessary and cook 5 minutes. Be sure to add a crab claw to each bowl of soup.

Serves 4.

Crab Lab Tip

The news today is full of articles touting the health benefits of fish and seafood, and Chesapeake soups and stews are a great way to include them in your meals.

West River Vegetable Crab Soup

This is best cooked slowly over a very low heat so that all the vegetable flavors can meld. Mom always said: Make the best vegetable soup you can make, then add the crabmeat and season to taste.

2 quarts vegetable stock

1 leek, white part only, sliced

2 medium onions, chopped

2 ribs celery, peeled and chopped

2 medium carrots, cut into small pieces

3 medium potatoes, cut into small pieces

1/2 cup chopped cabbage

1 cup green beans, cut into 1-inch lengths

6 to 8 tomatoes, peeled, seeded, and chopped, or 2 to 3 cups canned tomatoes

1 small T-bone steak

1 cup corn kernels

1 cup lima beans

salt and freshly ground black pepper

1 pound lump crabmeat

seafood seasoning to taste

Pour the vegetable stock into a heavy stockpot. Add the leek, onions, celery, carrots, potatoes, cabbage, green beans, tomatoes, and T-bone steak (whole). Simmer over low heat until vegetables are tender—about 40 minutes.

Remove the cooked beef. Cut meat into small dice, discard the bone, and return the beef pieces to the pot. Add the corn and lima beans and continue to cook until all the vegetables are tender—20 to 30 minutes. Add crabmeat and salt, pepper, and seafood seasoning to taste. Heat through, stirring gently, and serve.

Serves 6.

Crab Lab Tip

In my Crab Lab test kitchen, I always keep a pound of lump crabmeat on hand to dress up bowls of soup before they're placed in front of my guests.

Potomac River Crab Soup

Cream of crab soup, with its thick base of cream and its hint of sherry, certainly has its devotees. I'm one of them—in fact, I'm going to have a cup or two tonight. Why don't you join me?

2 tablespoons butter

2 small onions, chopped fine

1 pound crabmeat

2 tablespoons flour

4 cups hot milk

1 cup corn kernels, cooked

1 cup small lima beans, cooked

salt and freshly ground black pepper to taste

1 teaspoon Worcestershire sauce

1 cup whipping cream

¼ cup sherry

1 tablespoon chopped fresh parsley

Simmer the onions lightly in butter. Add the crabmeat and heat through. Add the flour and follow with the hot milk; stir slowly and let boil for about 10 minutes. Add the corn, lima beans, salt, pepper, and Worcestershire sauce; let simmer another 10 minutes. Add the cream. Before serving, add the sherry; reheat. Garnish with parsley

Serves 6.

Port Tobacco River Crab Soup

The right stock, tasty vegetables, and lots of crabmeat make a warm start to an autumn meal.

2 pounds tomatoes, peeled

2 teaspoons extra-virgin olive oil

2 cloves garlic, finely chopped

1 yellow onion, finely chopped

1 rib celery, peeled and finely
chopped

4 cups vegetable stock

1 tablespoon tomato paste

$\frac{1}{2}$ teaspoon sugar

salt and freshly ground black pepper
to taste

1 bay leaf

1 pound crabmeat

1 tablespoon chopped fresh basil

1 tablespoon chopped fresh oregano

1 tablespoon chopped fresh parsley

Purée the tomatoes in a food processor and pour into a bowl through a sieve to remove seeds.

Heat the olive oil and garlic in a saucepan over medium heat until fragrant, about 1 minute. Add the onion and celery and cook gently until soft. Add the tomatoes, vegetable stock, tomato paste, sugar, salt and pepper, and bay leaf. Simmer gently for about 20 minutes.

Add crabmeat, basil, oregano, and parsley, and remove bay leaf. Cook until slightly thickened—5 to 10 minutes—and serve immediately.

Serves 4.

St. Marys River Crab Bisque

The secret to good soup-making is taste, taste, taste!

2 sticks butter

3 cups whole kernel corn

1 cup diced onions

1 cup peeled and diced celery

1/2 cup diced red bell peppers

1/4 cup minced garlic

1 cup flour

2 1/2 quarts fish stock

1 pint whipping cream

1/2 cup sliced green onions

1/2 cup chopped fresh parsley

1 pound jumbo lump crabmeat

salt

white pepper to taste

In a 2-gallon stockpot, melt the butter over medium-high heat. Add the corn, onions, celery, bell pepper, and garlic. Sauté until vegetables are wilted, about 10 minutes. Whisk in the flour until a blond roux is achieved; do not brown.

Slowly add the stock, one ladle at a time, stirring constantly. Bring to a low boil, reduce to simmer, and cook 30 minutes. Add the cream, green onions, and parsley. Continue cooking for 3 minutes. Gently fold in the crabmeat, being careful not to break the lumps. Season with salt and white pepper.

Serves 6.

Crab Lab Tip

Call me picky, but I *must* use fresh corn and garlic when I make this bisque—and although red bell peppers are usually more expensive than green, they're also sweeter, so make them your first choice. Some of my friends must have Old Bay seasoning with this dish, so I put a shaker on the table to keep them happy.

Fish Soups

York River Fish Soup

Pamunkey River
Fish Soup

Piankatank River
Fish Soup

Rappahannock River
Rockfish Chowder

Mattaponi River
Seafood Soup

York River Fish Soup

There may not be a more welcoming and warming soup than one made with freshly caught local flounder or rockfish. I sometimes use a combination of both if I've had a good day on the Bay.

2 teaspoons butter

1 onion, finely chopped

1 leek, thinly sliced

1 carrot, thinly sliced

pinch of saffron threads

¼ cup white rice

½ cup dry white wine

4 cups fish stock

½ cup whipping cream

12 ounces skinless fillet of flounder or rockfish, cut into ½-inch cubes

salt and freshly ground black pepper

4 tomatoes, peeled, seeded, and chopped

3 tablespoons snipped fresh chives for garnish

Heat the butter in a saucepan over medium heat and add the onion, leek, and carrot. Cook, stirring frequently, until the onion is soft, 3 to 4 minutes. Add the saffron, rice, wine, and stock and bring to a boil. Reduce the heat to low. Cover and simmer until the rice and vegetables are soft, about 20 minutes.

Allow the soup to cool slightly and then transfer to a blender or food processor and purée until smooth, working in batches if necessary. (Purée the solids with enough cooking liquid to moisten them, and then combine with the remaining liquid.)

Return the soup to the saucepan, stir in the cream, and simmer over low heat until heated through, stirring occasionally. Season the fish with salt and pepper and add it, with the tomatoes, to the simmering soup. Cook just until the fish flakes.

Stir in most of the chives. Adjust the seasoning. Ladle into warm, shallow bowls, sprinkle with the remaining chives, and serve.

Serves 4.

Pamunkey River Fish Soup

This is a special soup packed with seafood in a rich broth. I sometimes add an extra pinch of red pepper flakes to my serving. I've learned that not everyone enjoys the additional heat, so serve it on the side.

4 tablespoons extra-virgin olive oil

1 medium onion, thinly sliced

3 garlic cloves, thinly sliced

1 rib celery, peeled and chopped

1 teaspoon chopped fresh rosemary

1 teaspoon dried basil

2 medium carrots, peeled and thinly sliced

2 cups chicken stock

1¼ cups clam juice

1 cup white wine

2 tomatoes, diced

1 red potato, diced

2 pounds assorted whitefish and shrimp

8 clams

pinch of red pepper flakes

salt and freshly ground pepper to taste

8 slices fresh sourdough bread

1 or 2 garlic cloves, peeled and halved lengthwise, dipped in extra-virgin olive oil

¼ cup chopped fresh parsley

In a large saucepan over medium heat, combine the olive oil, onion, garlic, celery, rosemary, and basil. Cook for 4 minutes. Add the carrots, chicken stock, clam juice, white wine, tomatoes, potato, fish and shrimp, clams, and red pepper flakes, and bring to a boil. Reduce the heat and simmer for 10 to 12 minutes. Season with salt and pepper.

Toast the bread; then rub the garlic cloves on both sides of the toast. Place a slice of bread in each bowl. Ladle in the soup and garnish with parsley. Be sure each bowl contains an opened clam!

Serves 8.

Crab Lab Tip

Never had fish soup? Here's a version that will make regular appearances on your table. Always buy clams from a reputable fish merchant. If you're using littlenecks (hard-shelled clams), choose those with even-colored and tightly closed shells.

Piankatank River Fish Soup

An old French proverb says, "Eat soup first and eat it last, and live till a hundred years be past."
Any flaky whitefish—or a combination of whitefish—can go into this smooth, creamy, white soup.

2 pounds mixed whitefish

1 onion, peeled and chopped

1 leek, sliced

1 rib celery, peeled and chopped

¼ cup white wine

2 tablespoons butter

2 tablespoons flour

½ cup milk

pinch of grated lemon rind

1 teaspoon chopped fennel leaves
plus extra for garnish

2 tablespoons chopped fresh parsley
plus extra for garnish

salt and freshly ground pepper to
taste

Put the fish, onion, leek, and celery in a large saucepan and cover with a quart of water. Bring to a boil and simmer until the fish is cooked. Lift out the fish and flake coarsely into a bowl. As you do so, return the skin and bones to the saucepan and continue to cook them with the vegetables for 20 minutes, adding more water if necessary. Strain the liquid into a clean saucepan and discard the vegetables and bones. Stir in the wine. Melt the butter in a small saucepan and stir in the flour; then gradually add the milk, stirring until smooth. Add this sauce to the fish liquid and cook for 3 to 4 minutes, stirring constantly. Then add the flaked fish, lemon rind, and chopped fennel and parsley and season with salt and pepper. Bring to a boil, stirring lightly, and serve at once garnished with a little extra chopped herbs.

Serves 6.

Rappahannock River Rockfish Chowder

Freshly taken from the Chesapeake Bay waters, a rockfish is a thing of beauty, with black spots that form longitudinal stripes down its silver sides. It is esthetically pleasing to view, and when cooked up in a chowder, oh, my!

3 slices bacon

1 cup chopped onion

1 cup boiling water

2 cups diced raw potatoes

4 cups stewed tomatoes

¼ cup catsup

2 tablespoons Worcestershire sauce

pinch of chopped fresh thyme

1 teaspoon salt

½ teaspoon freshly ground ginger

1 pound rockfish, cut into chunks

Cook the bacon, drain and reserve. Sauté the onion in the bacon drippings until soft. Add the water, potatoes, tomatoes, catsup, Worcestershire sauce, thyme, salt, and ginger; cover and simmer until the potatoes are tender. Add the fish, simmer for 15 minutes, and serve.

Serves 6.

Mattaponi River Seafood Soup

Once you master basic methods for making seafood soups, it's easy to invent a soup following a whim. I rarely have more than a vague idea of what I'm going to cook until I spot one or two special-looking foods—then the fun begins.

2 tablespoons extra-virgin olive oil

1½ cups sliced scallions

2 cups diced green peppers

1¼ cups diced onion

1¼ cups diced fennel bulb

10 garlic cloves, minced

1 cup white wine

1 quart fish stock

8 cups plum tomatoes, chopped and drained

½ cup tomato purée

2 bay leaves

salt and freshly ground black pepper to taste

20 littleneck clams, scrubbed well

3 steamed hardshell crabs

20 medium shrimp, peeled and deveined

1 pound rockfish or flounder

pinch of red pepper flakes

3 tablespoons shredded fresh basil

Heat the oil in a soup pot over medium heat. Add the scallions, peppers, onion, and fennel. Cook, stirring occasionally, until the onion is translucent, 6 to 8 minutes. Add the garlic and cook for 1 minute. Add the wine, bring to a boil, and cook until the volume of the wine is reduced by about half, 4 to 6 minutes.

Add the fish stock, tomatoes, tomato purée, and bay leaves. Cover and simmer for about 45 minutes, adding a small amount of water if necessary during that time (this should be more of a broth than a stew). Season with salt and pepper, remove the bay leaves, and add the clams. Simmer for about 10 minutes, and then discard any clams that did not open.

Separate the claws from the crabs and cut the bodies in half. Add the crab pieces, shrimp, and fish. Simmer until the fish is just cooked through, about 5 minutes. Add the red pepper flakes and basil and adjust the seasoning. Serve in heated bowls.

Serves 6.

Oyster Stews

James River Oyster Stew

Pagan River
Oyster Gumbo

Appomattox River
Oyster Stew

Elizabeth River
Oyster Soup

Chickahominy River
Oyster Stew

Lafayette River
Oyster Bisque

Nansemond River
Oyster Soup

Hampton River
Oyster Chowder

James River Oyster Stew

This is a delicious combination of flavors—perfect for warming your bones on a chilly winter day. I served it to my friend Bryan Hatchett one stormy December day. Bryan exclaimed, "Whitey, that's mighty good!"

1 pint oysters with liquor

1 teaspoon finely chopped shallots

2 teaspoons Worcestershire sauce

2 cups half-and-half

2 cups whipping cream

1 leek, white part only

salt and white pepper to taste

½ teaspoon lemon juice

paprika to taste

butter shavings

1 tablespoon julienned carrots

chopped parsley to taste

Drain oysters and reserve liquor. (You should have about ½ cup liquor.) In a medium saucepan, combine the oyster liquor, shallots, Worcestershire sauce, half-and-half, and cream. Heat gently until bubbles appear around the sides. Do not boil.

Add the oysters, leeks, salt, pepper, and lemon juice to the oyster liquid mixture. Heat gently until the edges of the oysters curl and bubbles appear at the edge of the pan—about 10 minutes. Do not boil. Add paprika, butter shavings, carrots, and parsley to garnish.

Serves 4.

Pagan River Oyster Gumbo

When buying fresh okra, look for firm, brightly colored pods under 4 inches long. Okra is an essential ingredient in a gumbo, where it's used for both thickening and flavor.

½ pound lard or cooking oil

¼ pound pork sausage

¼ pound spicy smoked sausage

1 onion, minced fine

1 cup finely chopped green pepper

½ cup peeled and finely chopped celery

2 tablespoons finely minced garlic

¼ cup chopped fresh okra, blanched

1 cup flour

1 tablespoon Worcestershire sauce

2 cups clam juice

2 cups chicken stock

1 cup fish stock

1 pound shrimp, shelled and deveined

1 pint shucked oysters with liquor

2 bay leaves

salt to taste

Tabasco sauce to taste

pinch of filé powder

chopped scallions for garnish

In a large saucepan, brown the sausages in oil to render fat. Reserve the sausages. Add the onion, peppers, celery, garlic, and okra and cook until soft. Add the flour and Worcestershire sauce and stir until slightly brown. In another saucepan, heat the clam juice, chicken stock, and fish stock until hot but not boiling. Add these hot liquids to the vegetable mixture, stirring until smooth. Simmer for 1 hour, uncovered, stirring occasionally.

Add the shrimp, sausage, oysters with their liquor, and bay leaves and simmer for 10 minutes. Season with salt and Tabasco sauce. Remove from heat, discard bay leaves, and stir in filé powder. Serve over rice garnished with chopped scallions.

Serves 6.

Crab Lab Tip

Filé powder has a woodsy flavor reminiscent of root beer. It must be added to this dish after you remove it from the heat, because too much cooking makes filé tough and stringy.

Appomattox River Oyster Stew

All along the shores of the Chesapeake Bay, variations of this soup abound. I grow about one hundred leeks every year, and a good many find their way into my oyster stew. Serve with oyster crackers and a good white wine.

1 1/2 cups sliced leeks

1 large onion, finely chopped

1/8 teaspoon dried thyme, crushed

2 tablespoons butter

2 cups peeled, chopped potatoes

1 pint oysters with liquor

2 cups whipping cream

1 cup milk

2 tablespoons snipped fresh parsley

1/2 teaspoon salt

1/4 teaspoon freshly ground black pepper

In a large saucepan, cook the leeks, onion, and thyme in butter over medium-low heat for 15 minutes, stirring occasionally. Meanwhile, in a covered medium saucepan, cook the potatoes in a large amount of lightly salted boiling water until tender, 7 to 10 minutes. Drain.

Add the oysters and liquor to the leek mixture and bring just to a boil. Reduce heat, cover, and simmer, stirring occasionally, until the oysters curl around the edges, about 5 minutes. Add the drained potatoes, whipping cream, milk, parsley, salt, and pepper to the oyster mixture and heat through. Serve in heated bowls.

Serves 4.

Elizabeth River Oyster Soup

An oyster soup is simple to make, but you must pay attention to the ingredients and method. The oysters are best when briny and freshly shucked. The herbs are best when just harvested.

4 tablespoons unsalted butter

1/4 pound bacon, cut into 1-inch pieces

2 medium-size leeks, white parts only, thinly sliced

1/2 pound potatoes, peeled and thinly sliced

1 quart milk

6 fresh parsley sprigs

1/2 bay leaf

1 large fresh thyme sprig

1 large rosemary sprig

1 teaspoon sea salt

1/8 teaspoon cayenne pepper

pinch of freshly grated nutmeg

1 pint oysters, drained, liquor reserved

1/4 cup minced fresh chives

freshly ground black pepper

Melt 1 tablespoon of the butter in a Dutch oven over medium heat. Add the bacon and sauté until crisp. Using a slotted spoon, transfer the bacon to paper towels to drain. Reserve. Pour off all but 3 tablespoons of fat from the Dutch oven. Add the leeks and sauté over medium-low heat until completely softened, about 5 minutes. Do not allow them to color.

Add the potatoes, milk, parsley, bay leaf, thyme, rosemary, and salt to the leeks and bring to a boil over high heat. Cover, reduce the heat to low, and simmer very gently until the potatoes are tender, 12 to 15 minutes. Remove the herb sprigs and bay leaf and discard. In a food processor, purée the mixture a ladle or two at a time until very smooth. Return the purée to the pot and reheat slowly.

Add the cayenne, nutmeg, and reserved oyster liquor. Simmer over low heat for 5 minutes to blend the flavors. Poach the oysters in the simmering soup over very low heat until they are barely cooked, 10 to 15 seconds. Adjust seasoning and stir in the remaining 3 tablespoons of butter. Sprinkle with the reserved bacon pieces and the chives. Pass the pepper grinder at the table.

Serves 4.

43

Chickahominy River Oyster Stew

Along the shores of the Chickahominy River at the time of Jamestown's settlement lived Chickahominy Indians, who were among those who took captain John Smith prisoner. Perhaps they fed him this oyster stew.

1 pint oysters with liquor

1 bottle (8 ounces) clam juice

1 tablespoon hot water

¼ teaspoon crushed saffron

1 tablespoon butter

1 cup coarsely chopped red onion

1 cup peeled and coarsely chopped celery

¼ cup flour

¾ teaspoon ground coriander seeds

3 cups half-and-half

¼ cup chopped fresh flat-leaf parsley

¼ teaspoon salt

⅛ teaspoon ground cayenne pepper

Drain the oysters in a colander over a bowl, reserving the liquor. Add enough clam juice to the reserved liquid to equal 1 cup; set aside. Coarsely chop the oysters. Combine the hot water and saffron in a small bowl and set aside.

Melt the butter in a large saucepan over medium heat. Add the onion and celery and cook for 5 minutes, stirring frequently. Stir in the flour and coriander seeds and cook for 1 minute. Add the clam juice mixture, saffron water, and half-and-half, stirring with a whisk. Cook until thick (about 10 minutes), stirring frequently. Add the oysters, parsley, salt, and pepper. Cook until the edges of oysters curl.

Serves 6.

Crab Lab Tip

Nothing nourishes the soul better than a bowl of this steaming stew, piping hot and brimming with fresh, succulent oysters. Warm the serving bowls in a hot oven before bringing them to the table.

Hampton River Oyster Chowder

This soup makes a rich and elegant starter. Serve it in shallow bowls so that the oysters are visible, and make sure to warm the bowls so the soup will stay hot.

1 pint oysters with liquor

2 large bunches of curly parsley, stems removed

1½ cups whipping cream

6 garlic cloves, finely chopped

salt and freshly ground black pepper

1 ripe tomato, peeled, seeded, and chopped

Drain the oysters in a colander over a bowl, reserving the liquor. Bring a large saucepan of salted water to a boil. Drop in the parsley leaves and cook until bright green and tender, 3 to 4 minutes. Drain and refresh in cold water. Press with the back of a spoon to extract as much water as possible.

Combine the cream and garlic in a medium saucepan and simmer over medium-low heat until the garlic is tender and the cream has thickened slightly, about 15 minutes. Transfer this mixture to a food processor, add the parsley, and purée until smooth. Return the purée to the saucepan and stir in the oyster liquor.

Season to taste with salt and pepper. Simmer gently for about 5 minutes; then add the oysters and continue cooking until the oysters are just heated through—1 to 2 minutes. Remove the oysters with a slotted spoon and divide among 4 warm, shallow soup plates. Ladle on the soup and garnish with chopped tomato.

Serves 4.

Vegetable Soups

Chester River
Tomato Soup

Bush River Leek Soup

Middle River
Escarole & Rice Soup

Elk River Corn Chowder

Back River Potato Soup

Northeast River
Lentil Soup

Susquehanna River
Mushroom Soup

Gunpowder River
Beef Stew

Patapsco River
Garlic Soup

Chester River Tomato Soup

This soup became ready just 15 minutes after I had lunch—but I couldn't put it down. I ate four bowls. The last time I made this soup I used water and chicken stock in place of beef stock.

6 tablespoons extra-virgin olive oil

small piece of dried chili pepper crumbled

1½ cups 1-inch stale bread cubes

1 medium onion, finely chopped

2 garlic cloves, finely chopped

5 medium fresh tomatoes, peeled and chopped

3 tablespoons chopped fresh basil

salt

6 cups beef stock or water, or a combination of the two

freshly ground black pepper

extra-virgin olive oil to garnish

Heat ¼ tablespoon of the oil in a large pan. Add the chili pepper and stir for 1 to 2 minutes. Add the bread cubes and cook until golden, then remove to a plate and drain on paper towels.

Add the remaining oil, the onion, and the garlic to the pot and cook until the onion softens. Stir in the tomatoes, basil, and reserved bread cubes. Season with salt. Cook over moderate heat, stirring occasionally, for about 15 minutes.

Meanwhile, heat the stock or water to simmering. Add it to the tomato mixture and stir well. Lower the heat and simmer for about 20 minutes. Remove from the heat and use a fork to mash together the tomatoes and bread. Season with pepper and more salt if necessary. Allow to stand for 10 minutes. Just before serving, swirl in a little olive oil.

Serves 4.

51

Bush River Leek Soup

If you're in a hurry, you can purée this soup right in the pot with a hand blender; if you prefer a smoother, more refined texture, use a regular blender.

1/4 cup butter

1 pound leeks, cleaned and thinly sliced

2 onions, peeled and thinly sliced

1 pound potatoes, peeled and diced

1/2 cup flour

1 quart chicken stock

pinch of nutmeg

pinch of thyme

salt and freshly ground black pepper

3 tablespoons half-and-half

croutons to garnish

Melt the butter in a large saucepan, add the leeks, onions, and potatoes, and cook for a few minutes, stirring, until soft but not browned. Add the flour and gradually stir in the stock. Add the nutmeg, thyme, salt, and pepper. Simmer gently, covered, for about 40 minutes, then purée in a food processor or blender. Place in a clean pan and heat through. Just before serving, stir in the cream and garnish with croutons. This soup may be served hot or chilled.

Serves 6.

Middle River Escarole & Rice Soup

The slightly bitter-sour flavor of escarole is always welcome, especially as the main ingredient in this delightful recipe, in which escarole is combined with white rice, producing a wonderfully rich, flavorful soup.

1 medium head escarole

2–3 tablespoons extra-virgin olive oil

1 medium onion, chopped

3 to 4 cups chicken stock

½ cup uncooked rice

freshly grated Parmesan cheese

Clean and trim the escarole. Save the golden heart for a salad. Cut the dark green leaves into ribbons ½ to 1 inch wide. In a large pot, sauté the onion in the oil until the onion is golden. Add the escarole and toss until it is covered with oil and begins to wilt. Add the chicken stock and rice. Cover and cook until the rice is tender. Serve hot with grated Parmesan cheese on top.

Serves 4.

Elk River Corn Chowder

Both corn and potatoes found their way from South America to other parts of the world via North America. Dried corn was used for this soup before modern agriculture ensured the availability of fresh corn all year.

5–6 slices thick bacon, cut into ½-inch pieces

1–2 onions, chopped

4–5 medium potatoes, diced

1–2 cups corn kernels

2–4 cups half-and-half (use part milk if you prefer a less rich soup)

salt and freshly ground black pepper

Sauté the bacon pieces in a large, heavy soup pot. As it begins to render its fat, add the onion. Continue to cook over medium heat until the onion is wilted. Do not brown the bacon—it should just cook through. Add the potatoes, cover with water, and cook until they are almost tender. Add the corn and continue to cook until the vegetables are tender. Taste and add salt if necessary.

Add the half-and-half and heat through. Do not boil. Season to taste, and add a few grinds of pepper on top.

Serves 6.

Crab Lab Tip

Use farm-fresh corn in season to enhance this classic Chesapeake recipe. Making it is a breeze. Eating it is a joy. Two or three ears of corn will supply you with one cup of kernels.

Back River Potato Soup

This is my mother's recipe. When we were growing up and were snowbound, we usually had this soup and a grilled cheese sandwich for lunch.

2 medium onions, chopped

2 ribs celery, peeled and chopped

4 large potatoes, peeled and cubed

salt

4 cups half-and-half

freshly ground black pepper

fresh dill

Put the onions, celery, and potatoes in a heavy stock pot and barely cover with water. Add salt. Bring to a simmer, cover, and cook until vegetables are tender, 15 to 20 minutes. Add the half-and-half—enough to make the soup as thick or as thin as you like. Cook over medium heat until heated through. Do not boil.

Grind pepper on top, garnish with fresh dill, and serve hot.

Serves 4.

Crab Lab Tip

Potato skins contain many vitamins not found in the "meat" of the potato. I don't believe Mom Schmidt ever peeled a potato, but if appearance is important, by all means take the skin off.

Northeast River Lentil Soup

This is another soup I grew up with. I love the earthy, almost nutty flavor. As they cook, the lentils slurp up much of the vegetable-flavor broth, leaving a thick and hearty soup—add water if it's too thick for you.

2 cups lentils

8 cups water

1/2 cup chopped onion

2 cloves garlic, minced

1/2 cup chopped carrots

1/2 cup peeled and chopped celery

1/4 cup extra-virgin olive oil

1 teaspoon salt

1/2 teaspoon pepper

3 tablespoons tomato paste

2 bay leaves

1/2 teaspoon oregano

3 tablespoons wine vinegar

1/2 cup diced salt pork, fried

Wash and pick over lentils; soak overnight in 2 cups of the water. In a Dutch oven, sauté the onion, garlic, carrots, and celery in the oil. Add the lentils, the other 6 cups of water, the salt, pepper, tomato paste, bay leaves and oregano; bring to a boil. Cook 2 1/2 to 3 hours, until lentils are soft. Remove the bay leaves. Purée in a blender or food processor until smooth—or leave whole. Add vinegar. Garnish with crisp salt pork cubes.

Serves 8.

Susquehanna River Mushroom Soup

This is a very sophisticated soup that is ideal for entertaining. Use your favorite mushrooms—portobello or shiitake are favorite choices.

5 cups sliced mushrooms

¼ medium-size onion, sliced

3 tablespoons butter

1 tablespoon flour

½ teaspoon salt

½ teaspoon thyme

dash of pepper

2 teaspoons tomato paste

1 tablespoon lemon juice

4 cups half-and-half

Sauté the mushrooms and onion in butter until the vegetables are just tender. Blend in the flour, salt, thyme, and pepper; when bubbling, stir and cook for about 1 minute. Then blend in the tomato paste, lemon juice, and 1 cup of the half-and-half. Purée in a blender. Add the remaining 3 cups of half-and-half and blend until smooth. If you want an exceptionally smooth soup, force it through a fine wire strainer into the pan. Reheat to serve, but do not boil.

Serves 4.

Gunpowder River Beef Stew

Add your family's favorite vegetables to this stew. A great recipe for using leftover vegetables, too!

1½ pounds boneless beef stew meat cut into 1-inch cubes

2 tablespoons cooking oil

4 cups water

1 large onion, sliced

1 small leek, sliced

2 cloves garlic, minced

2 tablespoons Worcestershire sauce

1 tablespoon lemon juice

¾ teaspoon sugar

1 teaspoon salt

½ teaspoon paprika

¼ teaspoon freshly ground black pepper

⅛ teaspoon ground allspice

1 bay leaf

6 medium carrots, peeled and bias-sliced into ¾-inch chunks

4 medium potatoes, cut into 1-inch chunks

1 pound small white onions, peeled and halved

½ cup cold water

¼ cup flour

snipped fresh parsley

Heat oil in a Dutch oven over medium-high heat. Add all the meat at once and cook, stirring occasionally, until it is brown, approximately 15 minutes. Drain the fat. Add the 4 cups of water, sliced onion, leek, garlic, Worcestershire sauce, lemon juice, sugar, salt, paprika, pepper, allspice, and bay leaf and bring to a boil. Reduce the heat and simmer, covered, for 2 hours, stirring occasionally.

Stir in the carrots, potatoes, and halved onions and return to boiling. Reduce heat and simmer, covered, until meat and vegetables are tender. Discard the bay leaf.

In a screw-top jar, combine the ½ cup cold water and flour, cover, and shake until smooth. Add this mixture to the stew and cook, stirring, over medium heat until thickened and bubbly. Adjust seasoning. Spoon stew into bowls and sprinkle each serving with parsley.

Serves 6.

Patapsco River Garlic Soup

"Surely one of the greatest satisfactions of life is to cook a really delicious meal, a meal that nourishes the body and cheers the spirit, and may be remembered with pleasure for a long time to come."

—ROSE ELLIOT, *THE FESTIVE VEGETARIAN*

2 tablespoons peanut oil

1 leek, white and tender green parts only, halved lengthwise and cut into 1-inch pieces

1 medium onion, coarsely chopped

8 to 10 garlic cloves, peeled and crushed

2 cups chicken stock

1 pound potatoes, peeled and cut into chunks

1 teaspoon salt

½ teaspoon white pepper

2 cups water

2 slices white sandwich bread, crusts removed, cut into ½-inch cubes

1 tablespoon canola oil

1 cup milk

garlic scapes for garnish

Preheat the oven to 400°F. In a large saucepan, heat the peanut oil. Add the leek, onion, and garlic, and cook over moderately high heat, stirring occasionally, until just softened, about 2 minutes. Add the chicken stock, potatoes, salt, pepper, and water, and bring to a boil over high heat. Reduce heat to low, cover, and simmer until the vegetables are tender, about 20 minutes.

Meanwhile, in a medium bowl, toss the bread cubes with the canola oil. Spread the cubes on a baking sheet and toast them in the oven until golden.

Strain the soup broth into a clean saucepan. In a food processor, purée the vegetables with a little of the broth until smooth. Return the purée to the pan and stir in the milk. Bring just to a simmer over moderately high heat. Adjust seasoning. Garnish with garlic scapes.

Serves 4.

Index